AI Customer Retention System

Keep Clients Longer With Predictive Marketing

By Joe Correa

Published by Live Stronger Faster

Copyright © 2025 by Joe Correa

This book is for educational and informational purposes only. The author and publisher are not engaged in rendering legal, financial, or other professional advice. Readers should consult a qualified professional before making any financial decisions.

First Edition

Table of Contents

Introduction

The Hidden Profit Engine Most Businesses Ignore

Every entrepreneur dreams of growth—more leads, more sales, more customers. Yet, the biggest secret in business success isn't found in getting new customers... it's in **keeping the ones you already have.**

Customer retention is the foundation of long-term profitability, brand strength, and predictable income. Studies show that increasing customer retention by just 5% can increase profits by 25% to 95%. But most businesses spend 90% of their time and money chasing new leads while neglecting the gold mine sitting in their customer database.

That's where **AI-driven predictive marketing** changes everything. Artificial intelligence allows you to go beyond traditional marketing metrics and dive into the psychology, behavior, and buying patterns of your customers. It helps you understand *who* is likely to buy again, *when* they're ready, and *what* offers will convert best.

The companies winning today aren't just selling—they're *anticipating needs*. AI gives you that superpower. From Netflix recommending the perfect show to Amazon predicting what you'll need next week, AI retention systems quietly drive billions in repeat sales. Now, small businesses can harness those same tools with affordable AI platforms that work 24/7 behind the scenes.

Why Retention Is the New Growth

In the past, customer retention relied on guesswork—sending random discounts, follow-up emails, or surveys hoping someone would return. But in the AI era, you don't have to guess. Algorithms analyze real-time data like purchase frequency, engagement levels, and churn signals to *predict* who's about to leave—and what will make them stay.

When you integrate AI retention models into your marketing system, you stop losing customers silently. Instead, you gain a **predictive advantage**—knowing exactly who needs a personal message, loyalty bonus, or re-engagement campaign before it's too late.

Retention-focused businesses also grow faster because satisfied customers become brand advocates. AI tools can track customer sentiment across reviews, messages, and social media posts, turning potential complaints into opportunities. Imagine a system that automatically detects frustration in a customer's tone and triggers a personalized support message or apology offer—completely automated. This shift from reactive to proactive marketing defines the next generation of digital success. Growth is no longer just about acquisition. It's about building **relationships that compound in value**—and AI gives you the tools to do it efficiently.

The Science of Predictive Marketing

Predictive marketing uses machine learning to analyze data from every customer touchpoint—emails, website visits, purchases, reviews, and even chat interactions. By processing these data patterns, AI can forecast future actions:

- Which customers are most likely to buy again.

- Which customers might churn or cancel.

- What products or services each customer will respond to next.

- How much revenue each customer represents over their lifetime.

This is called **Customer Lifetime Value (CLV) optimization**—and it's the new metric that defines how businesses are valued in the AI economy. Instead of guessing your next sale, predictive marketing lets you *engineer* it.

With the right setup, you can automate reactivation sequences for inactive customers, upsell campaigns for engaged ones, and loyalty rewards for your biggest spenders. You'll no longer depend on seasonal promotions or social trends—your system becomes self-sustaining.

And here's the best part: You don't need a data science degree. Today's AI retention platforms like HubSpot AI, ActiveCampaign Predictive Sending, or Zoho Zia do the heavy lifting. You just need to connect the data, define goals, and let AI optimize the experience.

Personalization at Scale

The future of marketing isn't mass communication—it's **micro-personalization.** Every customer wants to feel seen, heard, and valued. Yet no human team can personalize thousands of messages or campaigns individually. AI can.

With natural language generation tools like ChatGPT and customer data platforms like Segment or Klaviyo, your marketing can adapt dynamically. For example:

- Emails are written differently for each customer based on their history.

- Offers change depending on browsing or purchase patterns.

- Chatbots recommend solutions in real time using past behavior data.

The result? Customers feel like your brand truly *knows* them. And when customers feel understood, they stay loyal.

Think of it like building a relationship. AI helps you remember every detail—what they liked, when they bought, what problems they solved—and keeps the conversation alive long after the first sale.

This emotional connection powered by technology turns one-time buyers into lifelong clients. It's the ultimate fusion of psychology and automation.

Turning Data Into Action

Data is only powerful when it leads to action. Most companies already collect massive amounts of information—email open rates, purchase data, social engagement—but they fail to *use* it.

AI retention systems transform data into *decisions*. They interpret patterns and automatically trigger the right marketing action at the right moment. For example:

- If a customer's engagement drops, the system sends a check-in message.

- If a client repeatedly views an upgrade page, AI triggers a limited-time offer.

- If sentiment analysis detects dissatisfaction, an alert is sent to your team for follow-up.

You move from *reactive analytics* to *predictive intelligence*. That's the heart of AI-driven customer retention.

Even small adjustments—like sending messages at the ideal time or predicting when a subscription might lapse—can drastically reduce churn and boost repeat sales.

With the right dashboards and predictive alerts, you'll always know what's happening inside your business ecosystem without endless manual tracking. The AI becomes your silent partner in growth—always watching, learning, and optimizing.

Building a Retention-First Business

Customer retention is no longer optional—it's the **core strategy** for building sustainable success. When you combine predictive analytics, personalized marketing, and AI-powered automation, you create a business that grows smarter every day.

This book will teach you how to:

1. Identify churn signals before they cost you revenue.

2. Build automated re-engagement sequences that bring customers back.

3. Personalize communication using AI-generated messages.

4. Track customer satisfaction through AI-powered sentiment tools.

5. Increase customer lifetime value through loyalty systems and predictive offers.

By the end, you'll have a fully functional **AI Customer Retention System**—a framework that runs 24/7, keeps your customers happy, and consistently boosts your profit margins.

In the age of automation, the most valuable business isn't the one with the most customers... it's the one with the **most loyal customers.**

Welcome to the next evolution of business intelligence. Welcome to *AI-Powered Customer Retention.*

Chapter 1: The Lifetime Value Mindset

In the fast-paced world of business, growth is often measured by the number of new customers acquired. Entrepreneurs chase fresh leads, launch ads, and create funnels designed to bring more people in. Yet, behind every successful and sustainable brand lies a less glamorous but far more powerful truth: real growth comes from *retention*, not just acquisition. This chapter introduces the concept of the **Lifetime Value Mindset**, an approach that shifts your focus from chasing one-time transactions to cultivating long-term relationships that multiply in worth over time. When you adopt this mindset, every interaction, purchase, and piece of data becomes part of a larger strategy to predict, personalize, and profit repeatedly.

The customer lifecycle doesn't end when the sale happens—it begins there. Too many businesses celebrate the first transaction and move on to finding the next client. But in reality, a single happy customer can bring 10x the value of their initial purchase through repeat orders, referrals, and long-term trust. The challenge is that human follow-up systems often fail because they're inconsistent or time-consuming. That's where **AI-powered retention systems** enter the picture. Artificial intelligence automates relationship-building by tracking engagement patterns, analyzing buying signals, and identifying when and how to reach out again. It's like having a digital relationship manager who never forgets, never sleeps, and never loses track of an opportunity.

Adopting the Lifetime Value Mindset starts by understanding the difference between acquisition and retention economics. Acquiring a new customer typically costs five to seven times more than keeping an existing one. This means every dollar spent on loyalty pays a higher return than dollars spent on advertising. AI allows you to scale that principle beyond what was ever possible before. By connecting data from your website, CRM, social media, and email campaigns, predictive models can assign each customer a **Customer Lifetime Value (CLV)** score—a forward-looking estimate of how much that person is likely to spend over time. This transforms how you make decisions about offers, ad budgets, and follow-ups. You begin treating customers as long-term partners, not short-term revenue sources.

With AI retention models, you can see who your best customers really are—and why they stay. The data reveals what drives loyalty, which products lead to repeat sales, and which touchpoints need improvement. For example, you might find that customers who receive onboarding videos are twice as likely to buy again, or that those who interact with your chatbot have a higher satisfaction rate. AI helps uncover these patterns without guesswork. Once you know what works, automation ensures it happens consistently for every new customer. Retention stops being random and becomes a measurable, predictable system.

Personalization is the second pillar of the Lifetime Value Mindset. Traditional marketing relied on broadcasting a single message to everyone. Predictive AI marketing flips that model entirely by tailoring messages, offers, and timing to each individual. When an AI system recognizes that a customer is browsing a product page again or opening emails at specific times, it adjusts the experience automatically. It might send a reminder, offer a complementary product, or deliver educational content that builds trust. Over time, customers feel understood, not sold to—and that's what keeps them loyal. AI turns data into empathy at scale, allowing businesses to act with precision and warmth simultaneously.

The final step in this mindset is **proactive engagement**. Most businesses wait until a customer leaves to react—sending a "we miss you" email or offering a last-minute discount. By then, it's often too late. Predictive analytics can forecast when a customer is *about* to churn, giving you a chance to intervene in advance. For instance, if engagement levels drop or spending patterns change, AI can trigger a special offer, a check-in message, or a new content sequence designed to reignite interest. This keeps relationships alive and profitable. It's not about manipulating behavior—it's about maintaining relevance, which is the foundation of retention.

When you combine automation, analytics, and empathy, you create a powerful ecosystem that strengthens with every interaction. You stop chasing customers and start nurturing them. You stop depending on luck and start building predictability. This is the future of smart business—the evolution from growth through hustle to growth through intelligence. The AI-powered Lifetime Value Mindset doesn't just keep clients longer; it makes every client worth more over time. That's how you turn a business into a compounding asset—one where relationships, not advertisements, drive long-term wealth.

The Shop That Never Forgot

When Ava opened her small coffee shop in Austin, she had one simple dream—to create a place where people could feel at home while getting their daily caffeine fix. The first few months were full of excitement and growth. She launched social media ads, offered free samples, and worked tirelessly to attract new customers. It worked. Lines formed outside her shop every morning, and by the third month, she felt unstoppable. But by month six, something strange began to happen—her loyal customers started disappearing. She was still getting new faces daily, but fewer of the regulars were coming back.

She tried the usual tricks: loyalty cards, punch stamps, happy hour discounts. Yet, nothing stuck. People seemed to love her coffee, but they weren't returning consistently. "Maybe it's just the neighborhood," she thought. "People move on." But deep down, she knew something was missing. She was chasing growth in the wrong direction—new customers instead of nurturing the ones she already had.

One night, while scrolling through business podcasts, Ava came across an episode about AI in small business. The speaker mentioned how large companies like Starbucks and Amazon used artificial intelligence not to find new customers—but to keep existing ones happy. "Retention is the real gold," the speaker said. "AI can predict when a customer is about to leave, before they even know it themselves." Ava paused the episode and stared at her screen. What if she could build her own digital memory—a system that never forgot a face, an order, or a preference?

The next morning, she started researching. She discovered tools like **AI CRM systems**, **predictive analytics**, and **chatbots** that could automate follow-ups and track customer behavior. It all sounded intimidating, but she was determined. With a small investment, she connected her point-of-sale data to a simple AI marketing platform. Within days, the system began identifying patterns she had never noticed. It showed her who visited most often, what they ordered, how much they spent, and—most importantly—who hadn't returned in over two weeks.

One name caught her attention: *David M.* He had been coming in almost daily for six weeks, then suddenly stopped. The AI platform flagged him as a potential "churn risk." Ava clicked "Send Personalized Message," and the system automatically crafted an email:

"Hey David, we've missed seeing you around! We just added your favorite—hazelnut cold brew—to our seasonal list. Stop by this week, and it's on the house."

David showed up the next day. Not only did he redeem his free drink, but he told Ava he'd been busy and simply forgot to stop in. That little reminder brought him back—and he became one of her most loyal customers. Ava was amazed. "If one message brought David back," she thought, "what would happen if I did this for everyone?"

Over the next month, she let the AI system take charge. It sent personalized thank-you messages, remembered birthdays, and even suggested new menu items based on what customers liked most. Her revenue began climbing steadily. The AI even recommended offering subscription coffee boxes for her top 10% of customers—the ones with the highest predicted lifetime value. Within weeks, those subscriptions generated more income than her daily walk-in sales.

But what truly surprised Ava wasn't the revenue—it was the relationships. People began replying to her automated messages as if they were written personally by her. One customer said, "It's like you read my mind. I was craving your matcha latte today!" In reality, the AI had simply analyzed the time of day and purchase history to predict the craving.

Months later, Ava looked around her coffee shop, now thriving and full again—not because of ads, but because of connections. She no longer saw her customers as transactions. Each person represented a living story, a rhythm of visits, preferences, and experiences. Her AI system didn't just help her sell more—it helped her *care better*.

She often reflected on what changed. Before, she thought marketing was about shouting louder than her competition. Now, she understood it was about *listening deeper*—and AI gave her the ears to hear what her customers couldn't say aloud.

Ava's shop became a local case study in customer retention. She even hosted workshops for other small business owners titled, "How I Used AI to Never Forget a Customer Again." When people asked her how she managed to grow during a time when so many small cafes struggled, her answer was always the same:

"I stopped focusing on getting more customers. I started focusing on keeping the ones I already had."

Her story spread beyond Austin, inspiring countless entrepreneurs to rethink how they measured growth. For Ava, AI wasn't a cold machine or a replacement for human touch—it was a bridge between data and empathy. It gave her the insight to show her customers she genuinely cared.

By the end of her first year, her repeat customer rate had doubled. What started as a simple coffee shop had evolved into a community—one built on connection, consistency, and care. And behind it all was an invisible partner—an AI system quietly watching patterns, predicting needs, and ensuring that no customer was ever forgotten again.

That's what customer retention looks like in the age of intelligence: not algorithms replacing humans, but humans empowered by algorithms. Ava didn't just grow a business; she built relationships that lasted. Her shop became living proof that in the future of business, loyalty isn't luck—it's design.

Chapter 2: Building Your Predictive Retention Engine

The foundation of every successful retention strategy begins with one principle: *you can't improve what you don't measure.* To build an AI-powered retention system that truly works, you need visibility into every stage of your customer journey—from the first interaction to post-purchase engagement. This visibility becomes your **predictive retention engine**, a living system that learns from behavior, anticipates needs, and acts before opportunities slip away. In this chapter, you'll learn how to structure that system step by step: collecting the right data, connecting it across platforms, training your AI models, and automating the actions that convert insights into loyalty.

The first step is understanding what data actually matters. Businesses often collect too much information—names, clicks, locations, emails—but fail to focus on what drives retention. The key is identifying **behavioral indicators**, not just demographic ones. These are the small digital footprints that reveal intent: how often a customer logs in, which pages they visit, how long they stay, how quickly they respond to offers, or how their engagement changes over time. In the world of AI retention, these patterns are gold. They tell you who's losing interest, who's on the verge of purchasing again, and who's ready for a new offer. You don't need a massive database to start—just consistent, relevant signals collected over time.

Next comes **data integration**. Most businesses store customer data in disconnected silos—email lists in one platform, website analytics in another, and purchase history somewhere else. This fragmentation makes it impossible for AI to see the full picture. The solution is building a **unified customer view**, typically through a CRM (Customer Relationship Management) system that syncs data across every touchpoint. Modern AI CRMs such as HubSpot, Pipedrive, or Zoho CRM can automatically merge behavioral and transactional data. When combined, this unified profile allows AI algorithms to calculate metrics like churn probability, lifetime value, and satisfaction scores in real time. The more connected your data, the more intelligent your predictions become.

Once your data is centralized, it's time to teach your AI what to look for. Predictive retention models operate like digital intuition—they recognize subtle shifts in customer patterns that humans might overlook. For instance, if a customer who used to open every email suddenly stops for a week, that's a churn signal. If another customer clicks a "Learn More" button three times in a day, that's a purchase signal. These models continuously refine themselves using machine learning, improving accuracy with every new data point. Over time, your AI doesn't just report on what happened—it forecasts what's about to happen, giving you the power to act early and strategically.

But prediction without action has no value. This is where **automation** transforms insight into impact. Once your AI identifies a customer at risk of leaving or an opportunity for upselling, automated workflows trigger personalized responses instantly. For example, if a subscription customer's engagement drops, the system could send a check-in message or offer a tailored incentive. If someone buys a high-value item, an automated thank-you email might include a recommendation for complementary products. These touchpoints appear thoughtful and intentional, even though they're fully automated. The magic lies in the balance—technology doing the heavy lifting while your brand voice stays warm and human.

The fifth step is **feedback and continuous learning**. No predictive engine is perfect on day one. The secret to long-term success is allowing the system to evolve with your customers. AI thrives on feedback loops: the more it learns from results, the better it gets. This means analyzing which messages worked, which offers converted, and which customers responded best. Over time, your retention system will automatically adapt to market changes, seasonal trends, and customer preferences. What once required months of marketing experiments now happens continuously in the background.

Finally, your predictive retention engine needs a purpose beyond numbers. Retention is not just about reducing churn—it's about deepening trust. The more you understand your customers, the more value you can provide them. AI makes it possible to listen at scale, but what you do with that information defines your brand. Use predictive insights to surprise your customers, thank them for loyalty, and serve them better than before. When people feel seen and valued, they don't just stay—they tell others. That's how your AI system becomes a self-sustaining growth engine: every retained customer generates more revenue, more data, and more referrals, feeding the cycle of success.

By the end of this process, your business will have a clear, automated structure for retention. You'll know which customers are most valuable, how to keep them engaged, and when to act to prevent loss. The combination of prediction, personalization, and automation gives you a powerful competitive edge. You'll no longer rely on luck or reactive marketing—you'll operate with foresight. In the next chapter, we'll dive deeper into how to design **personalized AI engagement journeys**, where every customer feels like your only one. That's where retention evolves from strategy to art—powered by intelligence, guided by empathy.

The Gym That Predicted Loyalty

When Marcus opened his boutique fitness studio in Miami, he was determined to build more than just another gym. He wanted to create a space where people could find consistency, community, and confidence. His classes were packed for the first few months. New members poured in through social media ads and word-of-mouth, and for a while, it looked like he had struck gold. But by the end of the year, Marcus noticed a problem—his profits weren't growing. For every new member who joined, another one quietly left.

He couldn't understand it. His instructors were excellent, his studio spotless, and his classes innovative. Yet, his churn rate was nearly 40%. "People say they love us," he told his accountant, "but they keep disappearing." He started spending more on ads, thinking that constant inflow would cover the losses. It didn't. His costs grew while his revenue flatlined. Then one evening, while scrolling through a small business forum, he came across a discussion titled *'Predictive Retention for Gyms.'*

The post described how large fitness chains were using AI to identify members who were most likely to cancel. They analyzed attendance frequency, class engagement, and even social media check-ins to spot early warning signs. Marcus had never considered that technology could predict behavior so precisely. "Imagine if I could see who's thinking of leaving before they even tell me," he thought. That idea kept him awake all night.

The next day, he decided to build his own predictive system. He didn't have the budget for enterprise software, so he started small. He exported attendance data, membership payments, and engagement stats into a single spreadsheet, then connected it to an affordable AI tool that integrated with his CRM. At first, the data was messy—rows of numbers and timestamps that didn't mean much. But once the system processed everything, the patterns were undeniable.

The AI dashboard highlighted members in red, orange, and green: red for high churn risk, orange for moderate risk, and green for loyal clients. The system also explained *why*. One member, Sofia, had skipped her usual Monday yoga classes for three weeks straight. Another, Trevor, had opened promotional emails but hadn't booked a session. Marcus realized that these weren't random numbers—they were silent cries for attention.

The AI even suggested actions. It recommended that Sofia receive a personalized message offering a free guest pass for a friend. Trevor, on the other hand, should get a limited-time discount for his favorite class, spin cycling. Marcus followed the suggestions immediately.

Two days later, Sofia showed up with her sister. "I got your message just when I needed it," she said. "Life got busy, but this gave me a reason to come back." Trevor booked two sessions that same week. That's when Marcus understood what *predictive retention* really meant—it wasn't about selling more, it was about caring sooner.

Over the following months, Marcus refined the system. Every week, his AI dashboard updated automatically, showing him who needed attention and what kind. When engagement dropped, the AI triggered pre-written messages that sounded personal but were fully automated. It even learned the tone that resonated most with each customer—some responded best to motivational encouragement, others to simple reminders or rewards.

Soon, the results became impossible to ignore. His churn rate dropped from 40% to under 15%. Membership renewals hit record highs. For the first time, his revenue graph curved upward *without* spending a dollar on new ads. His team started calling the system their "Sixth Sense," because it could feel when a member was drifting away before anyone else could see it.

Marcus also learned an unexpected lesson: the AI wasn't replacing his relationships—it was strengthening them. Before, he'd only notice someone was gone when their membership expired. Now, he could reconnect with them long before they vanished. The automation didn't make things robotic—it made his communication *timely and human.*

His favorite example was Mia, a college student who joined during the summer but started skipping workouts in September. The AI predicted she'd cancel within two weeks based on reduced visits. Marcus sent her a message himself this time: "Hey Mia, noticed you've been busy lately. I remember how strong your goal was to tone up before graduation. Want to try our new express class? It's just 25 minutes." Mia replied instantly: "You remembered? That means a lot. I'll be there tomorrow."

That single message rekindled her motivation—and reminded Marcus why he started the gym in the first place.

By the end of the year, Marcus' small studio had become a model of intelligent customer care. Other gym owners began asking him for advice. He shared everything openly: "You don't need a fancy setup," he'd say. "Just data, a good AI engine, and the desire to listen." He even hosted local meetups for business owners interested in predictive retention. His new slogan, painted across the wall of his gym, read: *'We don't just train bodies—we remember people.'*

Marcus had turned numbers into empathy, and automation into connection. What began as a desperate attempt to stop cancellations became a movement within his business—a rhythm of anticipation, understanding, and care. His AI system didn't just save members; it strengthened the community that kept the studio alive.

For him, success stopped being about acquisition. It became about awareness—staying so tuned in to his customers that he could meet their needs before they ever had to ask.

Chapter 3: Designing Personalized AI Engagement Journeys

Customer retention is not a single event—it's an experience that unfolds over time. Each stage of a customer's journey offers opportunities to build trust, strengthen loyalty, and create emotional connection. AI allows you to design these **engagement journeys** with precision and personalization that would be impossible to achieve manually. This chapter explains how to map the full customer lifecycle using AI, from onboarding to renewal, and how to create automated systems that adapt to each customer's behavior in real time.

To start, you need to define the *path* your customers typically take. Most businesses have a natural rhythm—awareness, purchase, onboarding, engagement, and renewal—but few intentionally design experiences around each phase. Instead, they react to customer behavior after the fact. AI reverses this. It lets you anticipate what each individual needs at each stage and deliver it automatically. Imagine a customer onboarding sequence that changes based on how they interact with your first email or a reactivation campaign that triggers only for those showing signs of disengagement. This is what an AI engagement journey does—it listens, learns, and responds without delay. The first stage is **smart onboarding**. The moment a customer joins your ecosystem—whether through a purchase, sign-up, or subscription—is the most critical time to build connection. AI can automatically send personalized welcome messages, guide them through tutorials, and recommend products or services based on their specific goals. Instead of a one-size-fits-all email, your AI could say, "Hi Sarah, based on your purchase, here's a quick video showing how to get the best results," while another customer receives, "Welcome, Michael! Customers like you usually start with this setup checklist." These small touches make people feel seen and supported from day one, drastically increasing retention rates.

The second stage is **continuous engagement.** Once a customer is active, your AI's job is to keep the relationship alive. Predictive models analyze usage data, open rates, and interaction frequency to determine engagement levels. If a customer is highly active, AI can reward them with exclusive offers or early access to new features. If engagement begins to decline, AI can automatically launch a nurturing sequence—reminders, value-driven content, or re-engagement campaigns. Think of it as a personal concierge that never forgets to check in. The secret is consistency. AI ensures that every customer receives regular, relevant communication even as your business scales beyond what human teams could handle.

The third stage focuses on **anticipating needs before customers express them.** This is where predictive marketing reaches its full potential. Using purchase history, seasonal trends, and behavioral signals, AI can forecast what a customer might want next. For example, an online course platform might notice that students who complete a beginner course typically buy an advanced version within 10 days. AI could automatically send a personalized message offering a discounted upgrade at exactly the right time. This level of timing and relevance turns ordinary customers into loyal fans because it feels like your brand *understands them* intuitively.

The fourth stage is **feedback and sentiment analysis.** Retention thrives on listening, not guessing. AI tools can scan customer feedback, reviews, and even tone of voice in chat interactions to detect satisfaction or frustration. A sudden drop in sentiment triggers a human follow-up or automated reassurance message. For example, if someone leaves a three-star review, the system could automatically thank them, offer help, and notify your support team to resolve the issue. Over time, these micro-interventions build trust and prevent silent churn. When customers feel heard, they're less likely to leave.

The final stage of the journey is **renewal and advocacy.** Retained customers aren't just repeat buyers—they're brand ambassadors. AI helps you identify your most loyal clients and reward them meaningfully. You can automate referral programs, loyalty rewards, or early invitations to beta products. More importantly, predictive models can calculate when a customer is likely to renew or lapse and take preemptive action. For instance, if a subscription is due for renewal and AI predicts hesitation, it might trigger a "VIP renewal offer" or a "we appreciate you" message before they even consider canceling. This isn't manipulation—it's proactive appreciation.

To bring all this together, think of your AI engagement journey as an orchestra. Each touchpoint—emails, chatbots, ads, or messages—plays a different instrument. Without coordination, it's noise. But when AI conducts the sequence, every note harmonizes perfectly. Customers feel like you're always there when they need you, never when they don't. They receive guidance, care, and encouragement at the right times, which turns transactions into relationships.

Building these journeys takes planning, but modern AI platforms make it accessible to everyone. Tools like ActiveCampaign, ManyChat, Intercom, and Klaviyo now include predictive segmentation and automated journeys powered by AI. You can start small—one sequence, one behavior trigger, one feedback loop—and expand from there.

The goal isn't complexity; it's *connection at scale*. The technology is simply the bridge. In essence, a personalized AI engagement journey transforms how customers experience your brand. Instead of random marketing messages, they receive guidance that feels personal. Instead of being forgotten after purchase, they're continuously valued. When done right, this system becomes your silent retention engine—nurturing customers, generating referrals, and compounding loyalty automatically. This is how AI transforms retention from a marketing tactic into a living, breathing customer experience.

The Boutique That Spoke Every Customer's Language

Sofia owned a small online boutique that specialized in handmade jewelry. Every piece was crafted with care, each product description written with love. At first, her business grew quickly. Influencers tagged her on Instagram, orders came pouring in, and customers raved about the quality. But after a few months, the excitement faded. Her repeat sales were almost nonexistent. People bought once, complimented her designs, and vanished. She thought it was normal—"That's just how e-commerce works," she told herself. But deep down, she wondered if there was a better way to keep the connection alive after the sale.

One night, while packing orders late, she came across a webinar titled *"Personalization at Scale: How AI Builds*

Brand Loyalty." Out of curiosity, she clicked. The presenter said something that stuck with her: *"People don't leave brands because they don't like them—they leave because they feel unseen."* Sofia paused the video and stared at her order list. Hundreds of names, all of whom she barely knew. That's when she decided to build an AI engagement system that could treat every customer like her only one.

The next morning, she installed a customer relationship management (CRM) platform integrated with AI. It could track purchase history, website activity, and even browsing behavior. She spent a full week connecting her store data, email list, and social channels. When it was ready, the AI created something she had never seen before: *journeys.* It showed her how customers moved from discovery to purchase, where they dropped off, and when they typically returned—if at all.

Sofia started by redesigning her onboarding process. Instead of a generic "Thank you for your purchase" email, her AI-generated messages changed based on the customer's choice. If someone bought a silver bracelet, they received a message titled, "How to Care for Your Silver Jewelry So It Shines Forever." If they bought a gold necklace, it said, "The Secret to Keeping Gold Timeless." The AI even adjusted tone and color palette in the email to match the product's style. Within a week, her open rates tripled.

Encouraged, she took things further. The AI analyzed customer behavior and noticed patterns she hadn't seen. Customers who bought during weekends often returned to browse on Wednesdays. So, the system automatically sent those customers a mid-week "New Arrivals" email. For her most engaged buyers, it suggested limited-time previews of upcoming collections. For those who hadn't visited in 30 days, it crafted warm check-in messages like, "We've missed you! Here's a special gift to brighten your week." These weren't random promotions—they were perfectly timed conversations.

But what truly amazed Sofia was when the AI started predicting what people wanted before they asked. It noticed that customers who bought rose gold rings in February often returned in March for matching earrings. So, it began sending personalized recommendations exactly two weeks later. One day, a customer named Hannah replied, "You read my mind—I was literally looking for earrings to match this ring!" Sofia smiled, realizing that her AI had created something rare in online retail: genuine connection.

She also used the AI's sentiment analysis to understand how customers *felt*. It scanned feedback, reviews, and even

Instagram comments. When someone wrote, "Love the design, but the clasp was loose," the system automatically sent them a friendly message offering a replacement. When a customer left a glowing review, it thanked them personally and invited them to join the "Insider Circle"—a loyalty club the AI helped her create for repeat buyers. Those small gestures built trust faster than any ad campaign ever could.

After three months, her repeat purchase rate skyrocketed. Nearly 40% of her customers had made at least two additional purchases. But more than that, Sofia noticed something deeper: her brand was developing a soul. Every customer felt recognized, appreciated, and understood. The AI didn't just automate—it amplified her empathy.

She began naming her automated sequences as if they were team members. "Grace" handled onboarding, "Luna" managed engagement, and "Eve" took care of renewals. Each one had its own personality and tone. Her customers even began replying to them, thinking they were real people. One wrote, "Tell Luna I love her emails—she always knows what I want!"

One evening, as Sofia reviewed her dashboard, she realized she hadn't run an ad in over a month—yet her sales were higher than ever. Her retention engine had taken on a life of its own. The AI wasn't replacing her; it was scaling her humanity. It had learned the rhythm of her customers' emotions, desires, and timing. It knew when to whisper, when to encourage, and when to celebrate.

Sofia often told her friends, "I don't sell jewelry anymore. I sell connection." Her boutique had become more than a shop—it was a living conversation between her and every person who had ever clicked "buy."

A few months later, she received an email from a long-time customer named Lisa: "I've never met you, but I feel like I know you. Every time your message shows up, it feels like it was written just for me. Thank you for caring."

Sofia leaned back in her chair, smiling. That message wasn't for her alone—it was for the AI too. Together, they had turned automation into emotion, prediction into personalization, and data into devotion.

Her business no longer survived on first impressions—it thrived on lasting ones. And as she prepared her next collection, she realized something powerful: in a world full of noise, the brands that listen the closest win the longest.

Chapter 4: Turning Data Into Retention Intelligence

Data is the raw material of modern business growth—but without structure, it's just digital noise. What separates companies that keep customers for years from those that lose them after one purchase is how they use their data. This chapter reveals how to transform everyday customer information into actionable **retention intelligence** using AI. You'll learn how to track key behaviors, interpret signals of satisfaction or risk, and automate responses that deepen relationships rather than reactively chasing after lost clients.

The first step is to understand the difference between *data collection* and *data interpretation*. Many businesses proudly say, "We have all the data," but what they really have is clutter—thousands of touchpoints with no context. The power of AI lies in connecting these points to reveal stories: what motivates your customers, when they lose interest, and why they come back. Instead of measuring vanity metrics like clicks or followers, focus on the data that reflects *engagement behavior*—frequency of interaction, purchase timing, feedback tone, and response rate. These metrics show the rhythm of your customers' loyalty and help AI detect subtle changes before they become problems. Once you have reliable data, the next step is **feature mapping.** In machine learning, features are the specific attributes AI uses to make predictions. For customer retention, these features might include time since last purchase, product category preference, email engagement rate, or average transaction value. By feeding these features into predictive models, your AI can classify customers into segments—loyal, neutral, or at-risk—and assign probabilities of repeat purchase or churn. Modern CRMs can visualize these results on dashboards, letting you see at a glance where to focus your efforts. If you notice that high-value customers who don't open emails for two weeks are 60% more likely to churn, you can act immediately.

Next comes **behavioral clustering**, a powerful technique that helps you understand patterns across your customer base. AI analyzes millions of data points to group customers with similar behaviors, such as "frequent buyers," "seasonal purchasers," or "one-time deal seekers." Each group has its own retention triggers. For example, frequent buyers might respond best to loyalty programs, while seasonal customers might need reminders aligned with key dates. By tailoring campaigns to each cluster, your retention efforts become precise and efficient instead of generic. You no longer guess—you target with intelligence.

The fourth step is **sentiment and emotional analysis.**

Retention is not purely logical; it's emotional. Customers stay loyal when they feel understood and valued. AI tools can analyze the tone of customer messages, reviews, and even call transcripts to gauge emotional states. Positive sentiments might trigger automated thank-you notes or reward points, while negative signals prompt immediate human outreach. Over time, sentiment analysis creates an emotional map of your customer base—showing where your brand brings joy and where it causes friction. This feedback loop allows you to fine-tune experiences before they escalate into dissatisfaction or cancellations.

Once your data system is alive and learning, the next stage is **predictive automation.** The goal is not to just analyze, but to act automatically based on what the AI discovers. If the system detects declining engagement, it could trigger a "We miss you" message with a relevant offer. If it predicts high potential for upselling, it might send educational content that introduces advanced features or complementary products. The beauty of predictive automation is that it blends foresight with empathy—you're reaching out not because you have to, but because it's the right moment to reconnect. This creates a sense of genuine care at scale.

The final and most important element of retention intelligence is **decision feedback.** Every AI-driven system improves through feedback loops—the ongoing process of learning from results and refining its models. As you observe which campaigns succeed, which messages resonate, and which customers convert again, your AI adjusts automatically. This self-improving nature turns your retention system into a compounding asset—the longer it runs, the smarter it becomes. Over time, it will not only predict who will leave but also understand *why,* giving you the ability to adapt your business strategy in real time.

In the end, transforming data into retention intelligence is about creating clarity. Instead of drowning in reports and spreadsheets, you'll see your customers as evolving stories—each one with clear signals, preferences, and potential. AI becomes your translator, turning numbers into understanding and insights into loyalty. When you build this level of intelligence, you stop guessing what your customers need next—you *know.* And in the world of business, knowing your customers better than anyone else is the ultimate competitive advantage.

In the next chapter, we'll explore how to integrate all these insights into an **AI loyalty system**—a framework that not only rewards returning customers but predicts who's most likely to become your lifelong brand ambassador.

The Subscription Box That Learned to Listen

Elena started her business, *GlowCrate*, with one simple mission—to make self-care easy and joyful. Her monthly subscription boxes included candles, skincare products, and affirmation cards curated from small local brands. In the beginning, her idea spread fast through social media. Influencers shared unboxing videos, and her subscriber list hit 2,000 in just a few months. But soon after, she hit a wall. Her churn rate—the percentage of customers canceling their subscriptions—climbed to nearly 30%.

Each cancellation stung. Elena poured her heart into every box, but customers weren't staying. "What am I doing wrong?" she asked herself late one night while scrolling through exit survey responses. Most of them said similar things: "Loved it, but not sure I need another box." She knew they weren't unhappy—they were simply disengaged. The excitement faded after the first few months. That's when she realized the problem wasn't her product; it was her *connection*.

Desperate to turn things around, she started researching customer retention and came across the concept of **AI-driven analytics.** The idea that a machine could understand customers better than she could felt strange—but also intriguing. She decided to give it a try. She installed a predictive analytics platform that integrated with her Shopify store, email marketing system, and customer support chat.

At first, the amount of data was overwhelming—thousands of data points about customer orders, email opens, shipping preferences, and even the words used in feedback forms. But once the AI system organized it, patterns began to emerge. She discovered that customers who opened her "behind-the-scenes" emails stayed subscribed three times longer. Those who skipped the survey links in their first month were most likely to cancel by the third. And interestingly, people who posted their boxes on Instagram with hashtags tended to remain loyal.

With this new insight, she began to personalize everything. The AI created three customer clusters: *loyal fans*, *quiet buyers*, and *at-risk subscribers*. Each group received a different experience. Loyal fans got sneak previews of upcoming boxes and early renewal discounts. Quiet buyers received personalized messages showing how others used the products—simple storytelling to keep them inspired. And for at-risk customers, the system sent warm, genuine messages like: "We noticed you haven't opened your last box yet. Would you like a few ideas to make the most of it?"

One of those messages went to a customer named Nia, who

replied, "Wow, it's like you read my mind. I was thinking of canceling but hadn't had time to try everything yet." That message changed her mind.

As the months passed, GlowCrate began to feel alive. Elena's AI dashboard displayed color-coded insights—green for loyal, yellow for neutral, and red for at-risk subscribers. Every morning, she checked the dashboard like a weather report. If too many names turned orange, she'd review what triggered the shift. Sometimes it was a late shipment; other times, it was a box theme that didn't resonate. The AI didn't just point out problems—it explained *why* they were happening.

One day, the system alerted her that a spike in churn was coming. The algorithm had detected declining engagement in a specific customer segment—those who preferred minimalistic products. They had rated the last few boxes too "busy." Acting quickly, Elena sent out a survey asking for preferences and then used AI to design the next shipment around simplicity: a soft candle, a neutral-toned face mask, and a minimalist card that read, *"Stillness is strength."* The result? Not only did cancellations drop, but many previous customers reactivated their subscriptions after seeing photos of the new box online.

What amazed Elena most wasn't the technology—it was how human the whole process began to feel. Her AI system didn't just analyze numbers; it taught her to *listen*. The data revealed emotions behind the behavior. When engagement dropped, it wasn't laziness—it was a loss of excitement. When customers stayed silent, it wasn't indifference—it was confusion about how to use what they'd received.

To make that connection deeper, she added a new feature: personalized notes written by AI but reviewed by her before sending. Each note referenced the customer's preferences. "Hi Grace, since you loved last month's lavender candle, we think you'll enjoy this month's eucalyptus blend." Customers began replying to those notes as if they were handwritten.

Six months later, Elena's churn rate had fallen below 10%. Her subscriber count grew steadily without additional ad spend. The AI had evolved into her silent partner—an invisible team member that noticed what she couldn't and acted before problems escalated.

But the most touching moment came when a customer named Mia sent an unexpected email. "I've subscribed to so many boxes before," she wrote, "but yours feels different. It feels like someone actually cares if I'm happy." Elena smiled as she read it, knowing that "someone" was both her and her AI assistant, working together in harmony.

She started calling the system her "Empathy Engine." It wasn't about replacing human connection—it was about scaling it. The AI gave her the power to notice every customer's journey, every shift in sentiment, every moment that needed a personal touch. What used to be random feedback was now a symphony of signals she could interpret and act on.

As she packed her next round of boxes, she realized GlowCrate had transformed from a subscription service into a living relationship network. Every shipment was more than a product—it was a conversation. And the AI, quietly learning in the background, ensured that conversation never stopped.

In the end, Elena discovered the real purpose of data: not to monitor, but to *understand.* Numbers were just the language of loyalty, and once she learned to translate them, her business found its rhythm again—a rhythm built on anticipation, empathy, and connection that no spreadsheet alone could ever show.

Chapter 5: Building the AI Loyalty Loop

The most successful businesses in the world share one defining trait—they turn customers into advocates. While acquisition wins attention and retention sustains revenue, *loyalty* compounds growth. Loyalty is not simply a reward program or points-based system; it's a relationship built on trust, anticipation, and continuous value. This chapter will show you how to create an **AI Loyalty Loop**, a dynamic system that learns from each customer interaction, strengthens engagement, and transforms satisfied clients into brand promoters automatically.

The first step in building an AI loyalty loop is understanding its purpose: *to keep customers emotionally invested in your brand experience.* Loyalty begins the moment a customer feels appreciated. AI gives you the ability to make that appreciation personal and timely. Instead of sending generic "thank you" messages, you can use predictive analytics to recognize milestones—like 30 days since their first purchase, six months of membership, or their fifth referral—and respond in meaningful ways. For example, your system might automatically send a message that says, "We noticed you've been with us for 6 months—thank you! Here's an exclusive gift for being part of our journey." These gestures, delivered at the right moment, reinforce emotional bonds that traditional marketing can't replicate.

Next, design your loyalty loop around *behavioral triggers*, not just transactions. Many traditional loyalty systems reward only purchases, but modern retention models reward engagement. AI can track micro-behaviors like email clicks, social media comments, survey completions, or even time spent on your website. Each of these actions can contribute to a dynamic loyalty score. When AI detects consistent engagement, it can automatically escalate rewards—exclusive access, recognition badges, or early previews. When engagement drops, the system can gently re-engage customers with content or incentives tailored to their interests. This keeps your loyalty engine active and self-correcting.

Another key component of the AI loyalty loop is **predictive personalization.** Instead of offering the same incentives to everyone, your AI system should recommend rewards based on what each customer values most. Some might respond best to discounts, while others prefer exclusivity or education. For instance, an AI analyzing purchase history might discover that customers who attend webinars are twice as likely to renew a subscription. It could then automatically invite similar customers to upcoming sessions. By matching motivation to personality, AI ensures every reward feels relevant and thoughtful, not mechanical.

To make loyalty scalable, integrate **gamification and community dynamics.** Humans are naturally motivated by progress, status, and belonging. AI can use these psychological drivers to keep customers engaged. You can build automated systems where customers earn levels, badges, or exclusive titles for continued activity. An AI-powered dashboard can track their achievements and send personalized encouragement like, "You're in our top 5% of contributors this month—thank you for your support!" This not only boosts retention but creates social proof. When customers see others achieving recognition, they're inspired to stay active.

One of the most powerful outcomes of the loyalty loop is *advocacy*. Once a customer reaches the "promoter" stage—where they actively recommend your brand—AI can identify and amplify their impact. It can automatically detect positive reviews, social mentions, or referrals, then reward those customers with recognition, exclusive privileges, or bonus incentives. Imagine an AI that sends an instant thank-you to someone who tags your brand on social media or refers a new client. These micro-interactions turn happy customers into brand ambassadors without manual management. Over time, advocacy becomes a natural extension of loyalty, creating exponential reach through authentic voices.

Finally, the AI loyalty loop thrives on feedback and adaptation. Every customer interaction—whether positive or negative—feeds the machine with new data. The system learns which rewards sustain engagement, which messages resonate emotionally, and which touchpoints convert loyalty into advocacy. As it improves, your brand evolves from transactional to transformational. Instead of customers feeling like they're part of a program, they feel like they're part of a movement. That's the difference between retention and devotion.

When executed properly, your AI loyalty loop becomes a living system—predictive, emotional, and self-reinforcing. It not only reduces churn but generates organic growth by turning every loyal customer into your marketing partner. AI doesn't just help you keep clients; it helps you celebrate them in ways that feel natural, consistent, and human. This is where technology and gratitude intersect—where automation meets authenticity.

In the next chapter, we'll explore how to connect your loyalty system with **predictive churn prevention**—so you can detect risks, save relationships, and maintain an unbreakable cycle of customer connection before problems arise.

The Coffee Subscription That Built a Tribe

Daniel ran a small online coffee subscription business called **Roast & Rise.** He sourced premium beans from Latin America, roasted them fresh each week, and shipped them directly to his subscribers. When he first launched, he was ecstatic—hundreds of coffee lovers signed up within months. Every order felt like validation that his passion could become a sustainable business. But by the end of his first year, he noticed something painful: his churn rate was climbing. People loved the first few boxes, then quietly canceled.

He tried the usual tricks—sending discount codes, flash sales, and reminders—but nothing worked consistently. The problem wasn't his product. His customers still wrote positive reviews. The issue was that they didn't feel connected. They didn't *belong* to anything. One night, Daniel stumbled across an article titled *"AI and the Future of Customer Loyalty."* It described how AI could create loyalty experiences so personal they felt handcrafted. The phrase that caught his attention was: *"AI turns customers into community."* That was exactly what he wanted.

The next morning, Daniel decided to build what he called his **AI Loyalty Loop.** He integrated his website, CRM, and email platform with an AI engine that analyzed behavior and engagement patterns. Within days, the system had already identified insights Daniel had never seen before. It showed that customers who read his "Roaster's Notes" email every week were 40% more likely to stay subscribed for six months. It also revealed that those who skipped the newsletter after three weeks were twice as likely to cancel. Suddenly, Daniel understood what was missing—he wasn't building a conversation, he was shipping a box.

The AI helped him design a loyalty program that wasn't based on points or discounts but on *connection*. He created a tiered structure—Bronze, Silver, Gold, and Platinum—based on engagement, not just spending. Opening emails, rating coffees, sharing feedback, or posting a photo of their brew earned members progress. The AI tracked everything automatically, sent recognition messages, and even assigned "Coffee Explorer" badges to active members.

Soon, customers started posting screenshots of their progress on social media. "Finally made it to Gold!" one wrote. Another commented, "I can't wait to unlock the next level!" Daniel smiled as he saw a genuine community forming around what had once been a simple transaction. The AI had done something remarkable—it turned routine communication into motivation.

To make the experience even more personal, the system began

predicting preferences. When it noticed a customer frequently reordering medium roasts, it suggested trying a similar blend from a new region. For customers who had gone quiet, it sent gentle reminders like, "Your morning ritual misses you—how about a surprise roast this month?" Every message felt perfectly timed, as though Daniel himself had written it.

One day, the AI flagged a customer named *Lydia* as a "potential advocate." She had mentioned Roast & Rise on Instagram three times in a month, tagging her morning cup photos with #RoastAndRiseTribe. The AI automatically triggered a special message: "Lydia, we noticed your love for our brews—thank you for spreading the word! You're officially part of our Platinum Circle. Enjoy a free month of coffee, on us." Lydia was so thrilled she posted about it, and her post brought in five new subscribers that same week.

That was when Daniel realized he no longer needed to chase referrals—his loyal customers were doing it for him. The AI detected advocates in real time, rewarded them instantly, and amplified their enthusiasm without Daniel lifting a finger. The system was learning the psychology of appreciation, and it was working beautifully.

Over the next few months, Daniel began to see how loyalty could be measured in emotion, not just retention. His customers weren't staying because of free coffee—they stayed because they *felt seen.* When their birthdays arrived, they received messages with personalized roast recommendations. When they reached their one-year anniversary, they got a digital badge celebrating them as "Original Roasters." The AI remembered every milestone and made sure no customer went unnoticed.

Soon, Daniel started receiving messages that melted his heart. One customer wrote, "I've never been part of a subscription that feels this human. It's like you actually know me." Another said, "I don't just get coffee—I get connection."

What amazed Daniel most was how invisible the technology had become. The AI wasn't a tool anymore—it was part of the experience. It had built an emotional rhythm between his brand and his customers. Every email, every recommendation, every thank-you note reinforced the same message: *You belong here.*

Within a year, Roast & Rise's retention rate had doubled, and referrals accounted for nearly half of new sign-ups. Daniel had built what marketers dream of but rarely achieve—a self-sustaining community that grew on appreciation, not advertising.

When people asked him how he did it, he'd say with a grin, "I stopped treating loyalty like a program. I built a relationship system instead." His AI didn't replace authenticity—it amplified it.

Looking back, Daniel realized that loyalty was never about coffee. It was about connection. His business had become a conversation that never ended—a circle of appreciation powered by intelligence and fueled by heart.

And as the AI continued to learn, adapting with every sip and every smile, it proved what Daniel now knew to be true: *technology doesn't create loyalty—empathy does. AI just makes it infinite.*

Chapter 6: Predicting and Preventing Churn With AI

In every business, no matter how great the product or service, some customers eventually drift away. But in the age of artificial intelligence, losing customers doesn't have to be a mystery—it can be a preventable event. AI enables you to detect early warning signs, understand the emotional and behavioral triggers behind customer loss, and intervene before it happens. This chapter explores how to build a **predictive churn prevention system**—a proactive framework that not only saves relationships but strengthens loyalty by showing customers you care before they even think of leaving.

The first step is to redefine what churn really means. Churn is not just cancellation—it's the *gradual decline in engagement* that precedes it. It starts the moment a customer opens fewer emails, delays a purchase, stops logging in, or interacts less frequently with your brand. These signals often go unnoticed by human teams because they happen quietly and sporadically. AI, however, sees the invisible. It continuously analyzes micro-behaviors and identifies patterns that predict disengagement. The earlier you detect these signals, the easier it becomes to re-engage the customer before they fully disconnect.

To implement predictive churn analysis, you need to collect the right data—specifically, data that reflects customer behavior over time. This includes usage frequency, response time to offers, support tickets submitted, feedback sentiment, and purchase history. Once compiled, your AI platform assigns *churn probability scores* to each customer. These scores tell you who's most likely to cancel in the near future. For example, if your average subscription customer logs in three times per week but one user drops to zero logins for five days, AI flags that as high risk. Similarly, if a customer stops opening your emails or reduces spending by 40%, the system triggers an alert for proactive follow-up.

The second step is segmentation. Not all customers are at risk for the same reasons. AI can categorize at-risk customers into different groups based on behavior. One group might show *emotional disengagement*—negative sentiment in reviews or support interactions. Another group might display *behavioral drift*—less frequent engagement or decreased purchase activity. A third might face *financial strain*, visible through declined payments or smaller orders. Each of these categories requires a different retention strategy. By understanding the *why* behind churn, you can address the root cause instead of reacting to the symptom.

Once segmentation is complete, the third step is automation—creating intelligent re-engagement workflows. These workflows are triggered automatically when the system detects churn risk. For example, if a customer's engagement drops below a certain threshold, your CRM might send a personalized message like, "We've missed you! Here's something new you might love." If the system detects frustration in a support ticket, it could escalate the case to a live representative with an apology and discount offer. The goal is to intervene early, personally, and contextually—before the customer makes the silent decision to leave.

The fourth step is emotional recovery. Retention isn't just about transactions; it's about restoring trust. Sometimes, customers leave because of a misunderstanding, delayed service, or lack of attention. AI can monitor tone and emotion in real-time through natural language processing. If a message indicates dissatisfaction—phrases like "frustrated," "disappointed," or "thinking of canceling"—the system can instantly flag it for human review or respond empathetically with a custom message. This ability to detect and respond to emotion turns AI from a mechanical tool into a relationship manager capable of rebuilding confidence.

Another essential layer of churn prevention is **predictive reward timing.** AI doesn't just identify risk—it can also determine when to deliver value. For instance, if it predicts that a customer is likely to cancel within two weeks, it can automatically send a loyalty bonus, such as an exclusive upgrade, bonus content, or a personalized thank-you. These moments of unexpected generosity often reignite appreciation and restore engagement. Predictive rewards show customers that your brand values them beyond the transaction, reinforcing emotional connection precisely when it's needed most.

Finally, the system must learn from every outcome. Every successful retention event and every failed attempt provides valuable feedback for your AI to improve. When a customer who was flagged as "at-risk" stays after receiving a targeted message, that data strengthens future predictions. When another cancels despite intervention, the AI refines its understanding of what didn't work. Over time, your churn prevention system becomes more accurate, more intuitive, and more human-like in its ability to preserve relationships.

Predictive churn prevention is not about manipulation—it's about awareness. It's a way of saying, "We noticed you before you slipped away." That simple act of anticipation builds immense goodwill. Customers don't stay because you chase them—they stay because you understand them.

When your business combines behavioral data, sentiment intelligence, and automated empathy, churn becomes less of a threat and more of an opportunity—a signal to reconnect, to listen, and to grow. In the next chapter, we'll explore how to integrate these insights into a complete **AI-powered customer lifecycle system** that balances acquisition, retention, and loyalty in perfect harmony.

The Streaming Service That Stopped Saying Goodbye

Amara founded **StreamHavenz**, a niche streaming platform for independent films and documentaries. She started it because she believed great stories deserved a home outside the shadow of Hollywood. In the early days, the platform grew fast—movie lovers from around the world subscribed to support her vision. But after the first few months, she noticed something troubling. People were signing up, watching a few titles, and then canceling quietly. No complaints, no emails—just silent goodbyes.

She tried everything she could think of: new promotions, better thumbnails, reminder emails. Nothing seemed to stop the churn. "Maybe people just finish watching what they want and move on," she told her developer one afternoon. But deep down, she knew that wasn't the full story. These weren't casual visitors—they were passionate film lovers. Somewhere along the way, they were losing connection.

One night, as she reviewed analytics for the hundredth time, she stumbled on an article about **AI-powered churn prediction.** The idea fascinated her: what if she could *see* the signs of cancellation before they happened? What if she could understand why subscribers were leaving—not after, but before? That question became the turning point for StreamHaven.

She integrated an AI platform designed to track user engagement. At first, the numbers looked like chaos—watch times, click patterns, email opens, ratings, reviews. But after two weeks, the AI started painting a picture. It showed her who was likely to cancel within 30 days based on one simple pattern: inactivity. Users who didn't finish at least one movie per week had a 70% chance of leaving by the next billing cycle. The AI also revealed something she never noticed before—subscribers who watched one film but didn't rate or review it were far more likely to cancel than those who interacted afterward.

Armed with these insights, Amara built her first **churn prevention workflow.** Whenever the AI detected someone whose engagement was dropping, it automatically sent a message that felt human, not mechanical: "We noticed you haven't watched anything new this week—here's a personalized list of hidden gems based on your taste." The recommendations weren't random; they were calculated by another AI algorithm that matched viewing behavior with emotional themes. If someone had watched uplifting stories last month, it suggested films with similar optimism. If another had binged documentaries about travel, it sent them "Journeys That Changed the World."

Within a few weeks, cancellations began to slow down. Subscribers replied to those emails, thanking her for the suggestions—some even said it felt like the platform "knew" them. Amara smiled every time she read those words. The AI wasn't just predicting churn—it was reviving curiosity.

Then one morning, the system flagged a long-time subscriber named *Ben* as "high risk." He hadn't logged in for nearly three weeks, and his last review was lukewarm. Instead of sending an automated offer, Amara decided to reach out personally. "Hey Ben," she wrote, "I noticed you haven't been watching much lately. I just added a film I think you'll love—it's a mix of history and humanity, exactly your style."

He replied within an hour: "I was actually planning to cancel today, but now I have to check that out. Thanks for remembering me." That one message reminded Amara that behind every data point was a person, and behind every pattern was a story.

Encouraged, she deepened the system. She taught the AI to read the *emotional tone* of reviews and comments. If someone used negative words like "boring," "slow," or "disappointed," the platform automatically sent them a recommendation that contrasted those feelings—something fast-paced, exciting, or inspiring. If someone praised a film, the AI thanked them and suggested similar titles. Every touchpoint became an opportunity to re-engage.

A few months later, churn had dropped by half. The AI had even learned to predict seasonal disengagement—when certain groups of users, like college students or teachers, paused subscriptions during busy months. This time, instead of letting them go, the system sent preemptive offers: "We'll hold your account at no charge until you're ready to return." When those months passed, 80% of those users came back.

The results amazed her, but what moved her most was the feedback. Subscribers began to describe StreamHaven as *personal, thoughtful,* even *alive.* One message stood out: "It's like StreamHaven misses me when I'm gone." Amara read it twice, realizing her platform had become something deeper than a service—it had become a relationship.

By the end of the year, her AI system had evolved into what she called her "Cinematic Guardian." It didn't just analyze—it cared. It listened to silence, interpreted emotion, and responded with understanding. Amara often joked that the AI had better intuition than most marketers.

When a journalist later asked her how she built such loyalty in a market dominated by giants like Netflix and Hulu, she answered simply: "We don't chase views—we protect connections. Our AI doesn't wait for customers to leave; it listens for when they stop feeling seen."

That became the guiding philosophy of StreamHaven—and the secret behind its success. The platform that once struggled with cancellations had turned goodbye into hello again, all because Amara learned that the most powerful form of technology is the kind that listens before it reacts.

And as her AI continued to evolve, predicting patterns she hadn't even imagined yet, Amara smiled knowing that StreamHaven would never again lose a customer to silence.

Chapter 7: Integrating the Full AI Customer Lifecycle

Customer retention doesn't exist in isolation—it's part of a continuous cycle that begins with awareness, matures into engagement, and evolves into loyalty. Businesses that understand this full customer lifecycle can transform every touchpoint into a moment of connection and every interaction into an opportunity for growth. In the AI-driven economy, this integration is no longer optional; it's the backbone of sustainable success. This chapter will guide you through building a unified **AI Customer Lifecycle System**, where acquisition, engagement, retention, and loyalty work together seamlessly to keep customers connected, valued, and growing with your brand.

The first step in lifecycle integration is **centralizing data.** Most businesses operate with fragmented systems—marketing software for leads, a CRM for customer management, and separate tools for analytics and service. These silos create blind spots. A customer might appear "inactive" in one system but highly engaged in another. By integrating all data into one AI-powered hub, you gain a 360-degree view of each customer's journey. This unified database allows your AI to track behavioral trends across every channel—social media, email, web interactions, and purchases—creating continuity and context. The customer no longer feels like they're interacting with multiple departments; they experience one coherent, intelligent brand.

Once your data is unified, the second step is **mapping the customer lifecycle.** Every brand's journey looks slightly different, but most include four core stages: *Attract, Engage, Retain,* and *Delight.* In traditional marketing, these stages are linear, but AI makes them circular. Instead of treating retention as the end goal, it becomes the foundation for re-acquisition—loyal customers become promoters who attract new ones. The AI tracks each customer's stage in real time and adjusts messaging, offers, and content accordingly. A first-time visitor sees educational content, while a long-term customer receives loyalty rewards or early previews. This adaptive flow ensures every customer feels seen exactly where they are.

The third step is **real-time personalization.** AI-driven lifecycle marketing replaces static campaigns with living systems that evolve based on behavior. Imagine a visitor who reads a blog post on "How to Save for a Home Loan." The AI automatically categorizes them as a prospective buyer and adds them to a tailored email series about mortgage options. Later, when they sign up for your webinar, the AI transitions them from the "interest" phase to the "engagement" phase, offering advanced tools or consultations. This process happens automatically, powered by behavioral triggers that reflect intent. Every communication feels natural, relevant, and personal—because it is.

The fourth step focuses on **predictive progression.** One of AI's greatest advantages is its ability to forecast what customers will do next. It can analyze previous journeys to determine how long customers typically stay in each stage and what actions accelerate or delay progress. For instance, AI might discover that customers who receive a follow-up within 24 hours of purchase are twice as likely to renew their subscription. With this insight, your system automatically prioritizes timely outreach for every new client. Over time, predictive progression turns your lifecycle into a guided path where each customer advances toward loyalty with minimal friction.

The fifth step is **continuous engagement and retention reinforcement.** Once a customer reaches the retention phase, your system should never let the relationship stagnate. AI tools can track declining activity and trigger subtle reactivation efforts before disengagement occurs. For example, if a user hasn't logged in for a week, the AI might send a message saying, "We've added something new you'll love." If sentiment analysis detects dissatisfaction, the system can alert your support team or send a reassurance email. This keeps engagement loops alive and organic—like a conversation that never fades.

The final step is **closing the loop with advocacy.** Loyal customers are the most valuable marketing force any brand can have. AI can identify promoters using sentiment scoring, referral tracking, and social listening. When these advocates are detected, your system can automatically invite them to share testimonials, participate in ambassador programs, or earn rewards for referrals. Their stories not only bring new customers into the lifecycle but also reinforce trust for existing ones. This turns your retention model into a self-fueling ecosystem—each satisfied customer becomes a source of new growth.

When your lifecycle system is fully integrated, something extraordinary happens: marketing and customer service merge into one continuous experience. The AI becomes a bridge between every stage, maintaining emotional consistency and operational efficiency. Customers no longer feel marketed *to*—they feel guided *through* a journey. Every email, notification, and message becomes a reflection of your understanding, not your agenda.

Ultimately, an AI-integrated customer lifecycle isn't just a tool—it's a living representation of your brand's intelligence and empathy. It adapts, listens, and evolves with every interaction, ensuring no opportunity or relationship ever slips away unnoticed. The businesses that master this will no longer depend on luck or trends—they will operate with foresight and emotional precision.

In the next chapter, we'll explore how to scale this system—how to turn your AI-driven retention and lifecycle models into an automated growth engine that expands your customer base, amplifies loyalty, and compounds your brand value over time.

The Marketing Agency That Connected the Dots

Olivia ran a small digital marketing agency called **NovaLineBridge.** Her clients were mostly entrepreneurs and small businesses who relied on her to manage their ads, emails, and customer engagement. At first, things went well—she built strong campaigns, generated leads, and delivered results. But over time, she began to see a pattern she didn't like. Some clients were happy for a few months, then drifted away. They didn't cancel abruptly; they simply stopped responding, lost excitement, and eventually moved on.

Olivia was proud of her creative work, but she realized something was missing—a sense of continuity. "We're amazing at getting people's attention," she told her team one morning, "but we're not amazing at keeping it." Her campaigns worked in fragments, not in flow. Leads were acquired, sales were made, but the relationship after that felt like a disconnected silence. She knew that if she wanted NovaBridge to grow beyond project-based income, she needed to think differently.

That's when she started exploring **AI-driven customer lifecycle systems.** She read that large companies like Salesforce and HubSpot were using machine learning to connect marketing, sales, and customer service into one intelligent loop. The concept fascinated her—what if her agency could offer the same seamless experience to small businesses? What if every lead, sale, and support ticket became part of one unified journey powered by AI?

She began by centralizing all her client data into a single CRM. Before, her agency used five different tools—one for email, one for social media, one for project tracking, one for invoices, and one for analytics. Her AI platform connected them all. It started mapping relationships between actions that had once seemed unrelated. It showed her, for example, that clients who scheduled two or more strategy calls within their first month were 80% more likely to stay for at least six months. It also revealed that those who didn't receive a progress report within 14 days were three times more likely to churn.

Armed with this insight, Olivia designed a **customer lifecycle journey** for every new client. It began with a personalized onboarding phase powered by AI—automated welcome videos, calendar scheduling, and customized strategy guides. Next came the engagement phase: the system tracked every client's campaign metrics and automatically sent milestone updates like, "Your ad just crossed 10,000 impressions!" Clients loved it. They felt informed, seen, and supported.

But what truly transformed NovaBridge was what came next—**predictive engagement.** The AI learned to anticipate when clients might lose interest. If a client didn't open project updates for more than five days, it triggered an alert. If email sentiment turned neutral or slightly negative, the system recommended a quick call or special report. Olivia began seeing retention improve almost immediately. Clients who once drifted away were re-engaging before problems even surfaced.

Her favorite part was the *advocacy loop*. The AI identified her most enthusiastic clients—those who opened every message, replied with gratitude, or mentioned NovaBridge online. It automatically invited them to join her "Insider Partners" group, where they got early access to new marketing tools and discounts for referrals. Within months, referrals became a major source of new business. For the first time, her company's growth felt steady and self-sustaining.

One evening, while reviewing her AI dashboard, Olivia saw something remarkable. A heat map displayed every client's lifecycle journey—green for active, yellow for re-engaging, and red for at-risk. Nearly all her clients were green. She clicked through one account, remembering how that client, a small fitness brand, had nearly canceled a few months back. The AI had detected decreased engagement and suggested a "Progress Boost" campaign—a personalized report highlighting how their campaigns had improved conversions by 22%. That single email not only prevented cancellation—it led to an upsell for a larger package.

But what moved Olivia most wasn't the revenue—it was the relationships. Her clients started sending messages like, "I've never worked with an agency that checks in before I even realize I need help." The AI made her more responsive, but also more human. It wasn't replacing her; it was reminding her to care at the right time, every time.

As her agency grew, Olivia started teaching other small business owners about the AI lifecycle model. She told them, "The secret isn't just getting customers—it's guiding them, step by step, so they never feel lost." She showed them how automation could feel personal, how data could be emotional, and how predictive insights could build trust before problems appeared.

Months later, a client named Marco, who had been with NovaBridge since the beginning, summed it up perfectly during a feedback call: "You don't just manage my marketing. You manage my motivation." Olivia smiled, knowing that was the ultimate compliment.

NovaBridge had evolved from a marketing agency into an *intelligent relationship system*—a business that no longer relied on chasing leads but thrived on nurturing connections. Her AI didn't just help her scale—it helped her sustain. Every piece of data, every alert, and every automated message became part of a single heartbeat that kept her clients loyal and her business alive.

By connecting every dot, Olivia had discovered what most companies overlook—that true success isn't about building funnels, it's about building *circles*. Circles of attention, care, and communication that never really end.

Chapter 8: Scaling Retention With Automation and AI Systems

The moment you can retain customers predictably, your next challenge is scale. Growth through acquisition alone is expensive, unpredictable, and unsustainable. True expansion happens when your **retention system becomes automated, intelligent, and self-reinforcing**—when every customer interaction feeds data back into your business, allowing it to grow smarter over time. In this chapter, you'll learn how to use AI automation to scale your retention operations, maintain personalization at large volumes, and ensure that no customer ever feels forgotten—even as your base grows into the thousands.

The first step to scaling retention is **automated workflow design.** Automation is not about replacing human connection; it's about amplifying it. A well-built system uses AI to handle repetitive but vital tasks—sending thank-you messages, collecting feedback, recommending new products, or flagging customers who need special attention. The key is to define your *trigger points*—specific moments that activate AI actions. For instance, a "welcome" workflow might start when a new customer signs up, a "check-in" workflow might trigger after 30 days of inactivity, and a "reward" workflow might begin after a customer's third purchase. These sequences run automatically but adapt to individual behavior.

Next, you must master **personalization at scale.** Many businesses fear that automation makes communication feel robotic. AI solves that problem by using dynamic data inputs—details like purchase history, preferences, and engagement levels—to generate messages that feel unique to each person. Modern tools like ChatGPT, HubSpot AI, and Klaviyo use language models that can automatically write personalized copy for thousands of users simultaneously, maintaining tone consistency and emotional nuance. You can set up templates that read like human messages but are filled with smart variables such as "favorite product," "join date," or "most used feature." The result is a system that communicates with empathy—automatically.

The third step is **feedback automation and sentiment analysis.** Scaling retention means continuously listening to thousands of voices at once. AI tools can analyze customer messages, reviews, and survey responses in real time, categorizing them by tone, urgency, and satisfaction. If negative sentiment spikes, your system alerts your team or initiates an immediate follow-up sequence. This ensures no frustration or complaint goes unnoticed. Over time, the system learns which interventions work best and adjusts automatically. Think of it as a digital nervous system—sensing, responding, and evolving with every customer pulse.

Another essential layer of scalability is **predictive capacity planning.** As your retention systems grow, your resources—support staff, infrastructure, and communication bandwidth—must keep pace. AI forecasting tools can predict when demand will spike and allocate resources accordingly. For example, if the system anticipates an influx of renewals next quarter, it can pre-schedule support workflows or increase communication frequency automatically. This ensures smooth customer experiences even during rapid growth. Predictive scaling transforms chaos into rhythm—your operations move in sync with customer needs instead of reacting to them.

The next step is **integrating retention metrics into company strategy.** Many businesses treat retention as a marketing function, but at scale, it must become a strategic KPI across every department. AI analytics dashboards can track Customer Lifetime Value (CLV), Net Promoter Score (NPS), churn rate, and engagement levels—all in real time. These metrics should guide not just marketing decisions but also product development, pricing, and customer service. For example, if the AI detects that customers who use a certain feature have higher retention, your product team can prioritize enhancing it. When every department aligns around retention data, your business grows holistically—not in silos.

Another major advantage of AI scaling is **self-learning systems.** Each campaign, email, and interaction becomes new training data for your models. Over time, your AI learns which messaging sequences convert best, which offers reignite loyalty, and which channels work most effectively for different customer segments. This continuous feedback loop turns your business into a living organism—one that improves naturally without constant manual updates. The more customers you serve, the more intelligent and efficient your system becomes.

Finally, **human oversight** remains the soul of scaling. While AI handles the heavy lifting, human creativity and empathy ensure authenticity. Automation should empower your team to focus on strategy, storytelling, and deep customer relationships—not data entry. The most successful companies combine algorithmic precision with emotional intelligence. They use AI to *see* patterns but rely on people to *feel* meaning. When your technology and humanity align, you create scalable systems that never lose their heart.

In essence, scaling retention with AI isn't about doing more—it's about doing *smarter*. Your goal is to create a self-operating ecosystem that identifies needs, predicts behavior, and communicates authentically—all with minimal friction. When automation becomes intelligent, your business becomes timeless.

In the next chapter, we'll explore how to measure and optimize your AI retention system for maximum lifetime value—turning insight into ongoing profitability and ensuring that every automation, every message, and every experience contributes to long-term, compounding success.

The Online Course Creator Who Scaled Loyalty

Lena was a passionate educator who built her business around teaching digital marketing to entrepreneurs. Her first few online courses sold surprisingly well. She poured her heart into creating videos, templates, and community groups. Students loved her energy and practical advice, but as her audience grew, something unexpected happened—her retention began to slip.

At first, she didn't notice. Sales were strong, reviews were positive, and new students signed up daily. But when she looked deeper, she realized that many students never finished the courses they bought. Engagement dropped after the first week, and few ever joined her advanced programs. She was constantly promoting new courses just to maintain income.

"I'm working harder and harder," she thought, "but my business feels like it's running in circles."

One night, while watching a podcast on automation, she heard a guest say something that hit her hard: *"If you're rebuilding relationships every month, you don't have a business—you have a treadmill."* That was her wake-up call. She realized that real freedom would come from **retention at scale**—not just selling more, but keeping students learning, growing, and recommending her to others.

Lena decided to turn her entire education platform into a **smart retention ecosystem.** She connected her website, email marketing, and learning management system to an AI automation tool that tracked every student's journey in real time. The first report shocked her. It showed that students who completed 25% of a course were four times more likely to finish it, but those who went inactive for more than five days rarely came back. The AI even highlighted emotional cues from comments and surveys, revealing when motivation began to fade.

Instead of guessing, she now had visibility. She built a workflow where the system automatically sent personalized messages when engagement started dropping. If a student paused lessons for more than a week, they received a motivational email that read, "You're closer than you think! You've already completed 30%—let's keep the momentum going." For students who finished a course, the AI automatically recommended the next logical step, along with a "graduate discount."

But what really changed her business was **personalization at scale.** Each student began receiving lessons and updates tailored to their behavior. If the AI noticed that someone frequently rewatched video lessons, it offered them short written summaries. If another student preferred worksheets, it highlighted downloadable materials. "It feels like you know exactly how I learn," one student wrote. That was when Lena realized her system wasn't just managing students—it was *understanding* them.

As the months went by, she started automating every key touchpoint—welcome sequences, milestone celebrations, feedback surveys, and progress tracking. When a student hit 50% completion, the AI sent a "Halfway Hero" badge. When they finished, it congratulated them with a certificate and asked if they'd like to share their success story. Many did, and those stories became powerful marketing tools for new students.

Soon, Lena's small business began to feel like a living, breathing academy. The AI handled thousands of interactions per week, yet every message felt personal. Her support inbox got quieter, not because people stopped asking questions, but because the system was answering them automatically before confusion could turn into frustration. Then came her biggest breakthrough: **predictive scaling.** The AI forecasted when her student load would increase based on enrollment trends and seasonal spikes. It automatically adjusted communication frequency, added assistant workflows, and even pre-scheduled check-ins for busy weeks. What used to feel like chaos now felt like harmony. Her once-overwhelmed team could finally focus on coaching and creativity instead of chasing emails.

But what meant the most to Lena wasn't the technology—it was the transformation it enabled. One evening, she received a message from a student named Priya: "I've taken a lot of online courses, but yours is the first one I actually finished. It felt like you were walking beside me the whole way."

Lena smiled, realizing that was exactly what AI had allowed her to do—*walk beside thousands of people at once.*

Within a year, her completion rate tripled, her repeat student base doubled, and her monthly income became stable without constant launches. Her courses began selling themselves through word-of-mouth, fueled by satisfied graduates who felt genuinely supported. She called her new model "Education with Empathy," and other instructors soon began asking how she did it.

Her answer was always simple: "I stopped trying to do everything myself—and let AI help me care for every student like they were my only one."

Today, Lena's business runs on automation, but it doesn't feel robotic. It feels more human than ever. Her AI system scales kindness, motivation, and connection—proving that automation isn't about detachment, but about *remembering everyone, even when you're too busy to keep up yourself.*

By turning technology into empathy, Lena didn't just grow her business; she built a movement of learners who stayed, succeeded, and spread her mission far beyond what one person could ever do alone.

Chapter 9: Measuring and Optimizing Retention ROI

Building an AI retention system is powerful—but optimizing it for long-term profit is what turns intelligence into true impact. Every automated workflow, message, and predictive model must ultimately connect to one key question: *Is it increasing lifetime value?* Measuring and optimizing **Retention ROI (Return on Investment)** ensures that your system not only keeps customers but also compounds their value with every interaction. In this chapter, you'll learn how to track the right metrics, interpret AI-driven insights, and continuously refine your strategy to achieve sustainable, predictable growth.

The first step is defining what retention success looks like for your business. It's not enough to say, "We want fewer cancellations." Instead, set measurable goals tied to business outcomes. Common metrics include **Customer Lifetime Value (CLV)**, **Retention Rate**, **Churn Rate**, **Repeat Purchase Rate**, and **Net Promoter Score (NPS)**. CLV tells you the total expected revenue from each customer, while Retention Rate shows the percentage that remains active over time. Churn Rate is the opposite—the percentage that leaves. NPS measures loyalty through customer sentiment. Together, these metrics form your retention scorecard, giving a holistic view of how effectively your system nurtures long-term relationships.

Once you've defined your metrics, the second step is connecting them to your AI analytics platform. Modern CRMs and predictive marketing tools can automatically calculate retention metrics in real time. For example, AI can project future CLV by analyzing purchasing behavior, engagement levels, and communication frequency. If engagement rises, your predictive CLV increases; if it drops, the system can forecast potential revenue loss. By visualizing these patterns, you can quickly identify which campaigns, workflows, or customer segments are delivering the highest ROI and which need adjustment.

The third step involves **identifying your retention drivers**—the specific factors that lead to repeat business. AI helps by correlating variables across massive datasets. It can reveal, for instance, that customers who join your loyalty program have 40% higher CLV or that those who engage with personalized onboarding emails renew 20% more often. These insights let you double down on what works and reallocate resources efficiently. Instead of guessing which strategies are effective, you use data to invest intelligently.

Next, focus on **segment-based optimization.** Not all customers behave the same way or respond to the same strategies. AI allows you to measure retention ROI by segment—new customers, loyal advocates, at-risk clients, and reactivated users. By comparing retention performance across groups, you can see where your system excels and where it underperforms. For example, if reactivated customers have high churn after 60 days, your follow-up sequence may need improvement. Continuous monitoring ensures that each customer group receives the level of personalization and timing that drives loyalty most efficiently.

The fifth step is **automated performance testing.** Just as marketers A/B test ads, you can A/B test retention workflows. AI tools can run experiments at scale, testing different message tones, reward structures, or timing intervals to determine which combinations produce the best engagement and lowest churn. The system then automatically shifts resources toward the winning variation, ensuring ongoing improvement without manual oversight. Over time, your AI evolves into a self-optimizing engine—learning what keeps customers happy and adapting instantly as preferences change.

Beyond numbers, the sixth step is understanding **emotional ROI.** Customer retention isn't purely transactional—it's experiential. Sentiment analysis tools can measure how customers *feel* about your brand by scanning emails, surveys, reviews, and social media mentions. Positive sentiment growth often precedes retention growth. By tracking both simultaneously, you get a deeper understanding of your true impact. When customers express joy, trust, or appreciation, it's a signal your retention system is doing more than keeping business—it's building relationships.

Finally, optimize your ROI by closing the feedback loop. Use every insight to refine your retention system's strategy, content, and automation rules. For instance, if churn drops significantly after a new onboarding video series, update your AI to prioritize similar educational content. If predictive alerts consistently save high-value customers, invest in refining those models. This cycle of measure, learn, and adjust ensures your retention ecosystem becomes smarter, more profitable, and more human over time.

Retention ROI isn't about perfection—it's about progress. Even small improvements compound dramatically over years. A 5% increase in retention can yield over 25% more profit, and AI ensures those improvements happen continuously, without burnout or guesswork. When your system evolves automatically, your profits grow predictably, and your customers stay loyal effortlessly.

In the next and final chapter, we'll tie everything together by building your **AI Retention Master Plan**—a blueprint for running an automated, emotionally intelligent business that keeps clients for life while multiplying profitability month after month.

The SaaS Startup That Found Its Rhythm

Raj had poured everything he had into his software company, **FlowBridge**, a project management tool designed for creative teams. He and his small team worked endless nights building features they thought customers would love. They launched with excitement, gained hundreds of sign-ups, and watched revenue climb. But within six months, the celebration faded. Churn was creeping up fast—almost 40% of new customers were leaving after three months.

At first, Raj blamed competition. There were dozens of tools like his, each promising productivity and simplicity. But when he started reading exit surveys, he noticed a pattern. Most customers weren't leaving because they disliked FlowBridge—they were leaving because they *lost connection.* They didn't understand all its features, forgot to log in, or didn't feel supported. The product worked perfectly, but the relationship didn't.

That realization hit him hard. He'd spent all his energy building the tool—but not the trust. That night, determined to fix it, Raj sketched a new plan on a whiteboard and labeled it: **"Retention ROI."** If he was going to survive, he needed to measure not just growth—but *continuity*.

He integrated AI analytics into his system to start tracking what really mattered. The dashboard revealed truths he hadn't seen before. New users who completed onboarding videos within 24 hours were twice as likely to stay. Teams that created three or more projects within the first week renewed their subscriptions at a rate of 87%. And customers who joined his weekly "workflow tips" email series had the highest lifetime value. The data was clear: retention wasn't about discounts or features—it was about activation, education, and engagement.

Raj decided to automate everything the AI identified as a "retention driver." He built workflows that automatically sent new users short tutorial videos customized to their industry. If the system noticed inactivity after a few days, it sent an encouraging email that said, "Your next project template is waiting—get started in one click." Each message was tailored, timely, and human. The results were instant—churn dropped by 15% in just one month.

But Raj wasn't satisfied with reducing loss—he wanted to *maximize lifetime value.* He used AI to calculate **Customer Lifetime Value (CLV)** for each account, assigning scores based on activity, upgrades, and referrals. Then he segmented customers into groups: *New Starters, Active Users, Silent Accounts,* and *Power Advocates.* Each group received a personalized journey. Power Advocates got surprise loyalty gifts and referral bonuses. Silent Accounts received automated check-ins. New Starters were nurtured with onboarding success stories. For the first time, his entire customer base felt like a living ecosystem—each part cared for differently.

After three months, his CLV dashboard showed something remarkable. Average revenue per customer had increased by 40%, while churn had fallen below 10%. The AI had learned to predict behavior before it happened, alerting Raj when a high-value customer was at risk. One such alert came for a client named "Team Horizon," a design agency that hadn't logged in for two weeks. The system sent an alert labeled "High Risk – 72% Probability of Churn."

Raj personally reached out: "Hey Jasmine, I noticed your team's been quieter lately—anything I can help with?" She replied, "Honestly, we love the tool, but we've been too busy to update our templates." Raj quickly recorded a one-minute video showing her how to automate it. Not only did they stay, but they upgraded their plan the next week. That moment taught him that AI didn't just save accounts—it revealed opportunities for deeper service. Encouraged, Raj took optimization further. The AI started running A/B tests on retention emails—testing tone, timing, and subject lines. It discovered that messages written in a friendly, conversational style performed 28% better than formal ones. It also found that sending re-engagement messages at 10 a.m. on Tuesdays generated the highest click-through rates. Raj no longer guessed what worked—his system *told* him.

But the most transformative insight came from **sentiment analysis.** The AI analyzed feedback across customer chats, emails, and reviews, assigning emotional scores from "frustrated" to "delighted." Raj could literally see the mood of his customer base in real time. When positive sentiment dipped, he reviewed the cause—sometimes a feature bug, sometimes an unclear update. When it rose, he celebrated it with his team. The emotional metrics became just as important as financial ones.

Within a year, FlowBridge had turned into a retention powerhouse. The same customers who once churned were now renewing automatically and referring new users. Revenue stabilized, marketing costs dropped, and the company began compounding growth month after month. Raj called it his "invisible engine"—a system that ran day and night, building trust through automation, empathy, and precision.

One morning, while reviewing his dashboard, Raj noticed something symbolic. The churn graph that used to climb upward had now flattened to almost zero. The CLV line, once stagnant, was rising steadily like a mountain slope. For the first time, his company felt calm—predictable, scalable, and alive.

When asked by a friend how he'd managed such a turnaround, Raj smiled and said, "We stopped chasing new customers—and started caring about the ones we already had. The AI just taught us how to do it consistently."

The truth was simple but profound: FlowBridge hadn't become a tech company—it had become a relationship company powered by intelligence. Every feature, email, and alert now served one purpose: to make customers feel remembered.

Raj often looked at his whiteboard where he had once written "Retention ROI." Now he had added two more words below it: *"Measured in trust."*

Because what he finally understood was that numbers could measure growth—but relationships sustained it. And when you combine data with care, churn doesn't stand a chance.

Chapter 10: The AI Retention Master Plan

You've learned how to attract, engage, retain, and delight customers using AI. Now it's time to integrate everything into a single, cohesive **AI Retention Master Plan**—a blueprint that keeps customers for life and grows your profits predictably. This plan unites all the principles from previous chapters—predictive marketing, behavioral analytics, emotional intelligence, personalization, and automation—into one self-sustaining system that operates around the clock.

The first foundation of your master plan is **data unity and clarity.** Your AI retention system can only be as smart as the data it receives. Consolidate all customer information—sales, engagement, support, reviews, and feedback—into a unified CRM or data warehouse. Then, apply AI models that analyze relationships across every touchpoint. This creates a "single source of truth" for every customer. Your marketing team, sales reps, and support agents all work from the same insights, ensuring consistency and preventing disjointed communication. A unified system also allows AI to automatically detect when a customer is transitioning between stages—such as moving from engagement to risk—and activate the appropriate retention response. The second layer of the plan is **predictive engagement cycles.** Instead of reacting when customers disengage, design automated systems that *anticipate* needs before they arise. AI identifies micro-behaviors that indicate changes in sentiment or interest, such as slower response times, reduced logins, or skipped purchases. Based on these triggers, the system automatically initiates actions—such as personalized re-engagement messages, relevant product recommendations, or loyalty incentives. Predictive engagement ensures your brand feels proactive, not reactive. The goal is to make every customer feel as though your business always knows the right thing to say at the right time.

The third layer is **emotional automation.** Retention is not about cold algorithms—it's about empathy at scale. Emotional automation uses AI to interpret tone, language, and sentiment from customer interactions, allowing your system to respond in ways that feel personal and caring. For example, when a customer expresses frustration, the AI can deliver an empathetic message like, "We understand how frustrating that can be. Let's fix it right away." Meanwhile, a satisfied customer might receive a thank-you or referral invitation. Over time, your AI learns emotional context, adjusting tone and content dynamically. This bridges the gap between automation and humanity, creating digital experiences that feel authentically human.

The fourth component of your master plan involves **customer lifecycle synchronization.** Your acquisition, onboarding, engagement, retention, and loyalty strategies should not exist in separate silos. Instead, they should operate as an interconnected cycle where each phase feeds the next. AI-powered lifecycle orchestration ensures that when one customer completes a phase—such as a renewal—they're seamlessly transitioned into the next, such as loyalty or advocacy. If disengagement occurs, the system routes them back into the reactivation sequence. The result is a circular journey where no customer is ever "lost"—only moving between phases of connection.

Next, implement **automated performance optimization.** The beauty of AI retention systems is that they improve continuously through data feedback loops. Every campaign, message, and action becomes input for future optimization. You can set KPIs like Customer Lifetime Value (CLV), Net Promoter Score (NPS), and churn rate as live metrics. The AI measures performance, compares results, and automatically adjusts workflows for better outcomes. For example, if certain re-engagement messages outperform others, the AI increases their frequency and applies similar language patterns elsewhere. This self-optimizing mechanism ensures your retention strategy evolves alongside your customers. Another crucial element is **human oversight and brand**

alignment. Even the best AI systems require emotional intelligence that only people can provide. Your human team should review AI outputs regularly—especially during customer interactions that carry emotional weight or high-value decisions. The AI handles precision and prediction; humans handle empathy and ethics. Together, they create a balance between automation and authenticity. The brands that thrive will be those that automate efficiency without losing sincerity.

The final step of your AI Retention Master Plan is **sustainability and expansion.** Once your retention system operates efficiently, it becomes a replicable model across all your products and markets. You can expand it to new customer segments, languages, or regions with minimal friction. As your system scales, its predictive capabilities strengthen—the more data it processes, the more nuanced its understanding becomes. You move from managing customers reactively to nurturing communities intuitively.

To summarize, your AI Retention Master Plan consists of six pillars:

1. Unified Data and Clarity

2. Predictive Engagement Cycles

3. Emotional Automation

4. Lifecycle Synchronization

5. Automated Optimization

6. Human Oversight and Sustainability

When all six are implemented, your business achieves the ultimate balance: automation with empathy, prediction with personalization, and technology with trust.

Your AI Retention Master Plan isn't a tool—it's a living ecosystem that keeps growing, adapting, and compounding your results. It ensures your business is not just intelligent—but emotionally intelligent, capable of connecting with thousands of people in ways that still feel one-on-one.

In the next and final section, we'll bring this book to a close with a powerful story that illustrates how a single AI retention system transformed not just a business—but its entire relationship with customers—proving that the future of marketing isn't about machines replacing people, but about machines helping people *care at scale.*

The Brand That Never Lost a Customer Again

When Elena founded her skincare company, **PureGlow Botanicals**, she didn't imagine it would grow beyond her small apartment. She started with a simple goal—to create clean, natural products that made people feel confident in their skin. At first, everything ran on passion and word-of-mouth. Customers adored her formulas, and orders poured in. But as PureGlow expanded, Elena noticed something that made her stomach sink—customers who once raved about her products were quietly disappearing.

She didn't understand it. Her ingredients were top-tier, her packaging elegant, and her reviews glowing. Yet each month, her returning customer rate dropped. She felt helpless watching the churn creep higher. "What's wrong?" she'd ask her team. "Are we missing something?" But no one had answers. They were too busy managing the day-to-day chaos of fulfillment, support tickets, and product launches to spot patterns hiding beneath the surface.

Then one day, at a business conference, Elena attended a talk titled *"How AI Builds Customer Loyalty at Scale."* The speaker said something she never forgot: *"Your business doesn't lose customers because of bad products—it loses them because of missed moments."* That night, she couldn't sleep. Missed moments—that phrase kept echoing. What if she could see every one of them before it was too late?

When she returned home, Elena decided to rebuild her business from the inside out. She connected all her platforms—Shopify, email marketing, customer reviews, and social media—into a single AI-driven CRM. Within a week, the system began generating insights that shocked her. It showed that customers who received a follow-up email within 48 hours of their first purchase were 70% more likely to order again. Those who interacted with her "morning routine tips" email series had an average lifetime value three times higher than the rest.

Elena realized she'd been running her business like a straight line—get the sale, deliver the product, move on. But her customers were living in circles. They wanted to be part of something ongoing, something that felt personal and evolving. That's when she created her **AI Retention Master Plan**—a system designed not to chase people, but to *care for them automatically.*

The first part of her system was data unity. Every customer's journey was tracked in one place, from their first click to their latest reorder. The AI recognized patterns she'd never seen—who preferred morning skincare versus evening routines, who bought during sales versus full price, and even who stopped ordering right before seasonal changes. Each insight became an opportunity to personalize.

The second layer was predictive engagement. When a customer's buying rhythm began to slow, the AI sent a soft reminder: "Hi Sofia, it looks like your favorite serum might be running low—would you like to restock before the weekend?" It wasn't spam; it was intuition. People responded with gratitude instead of annoyance. Many even replied personally: "How did you know? I just ran out!"

Then came emotional automation. Elena's AI analyzed messages, reviews, and comments to gauge customer sentiment. If someone sounded unhappy, it triggered a compassionate follow-up from her team. If someone left a glowing review, it automatically sent a thank-you with a loyalty bonus. Every customer felt noticed. One wrote back, "I can't believe how human your emails feel—it's like you're reading my mind."

Soon, PureGlow began running on rhythm instead of reaction. Every morning, Elena opened her dashboard to a single question from the AI: *"Would you like me to reconnect with 17 at-risk customers today?"* She clicked yes, and the system handled the rest—sending personalized offers, reminders, or care messages automatically.

Her customers stopped slipping through the cracks. Churn fell from 28% to under 6% in six months. Retention soared, referrals grew, and her revenue stabilized like never before. For the first time, she could breathe.

But the most extraordinary part came one evening when Elena received a handwritten letter from a long-time customer named Maya. "Dear Elena," it began, "I've been with PureGlow for two years now, and it's the only company that feels like it actually remembers me. You don't just sell products—you make me feel cared for. Thank you for that."

Elena read the letter twice. She smiled, realizing that her AI had done more than automate—it had amplified her heart. What once required constant stress and manual follow-ups now happened naturally, gracefully, and authentically. The system didn't replace her; it multiplied her capacity to love her customers at scale.

Years later, when other business owners asked how she built such fierce loyalty, she'd laugh and say, "I built an AI system that helps me *remember everyone*. That's it. That's the secret."

Her company had evolved beyond transactions—it became a living conversation, one that never ended. Every sale was a new beginning, every message a continuation, every customer a friend.

PureGlow had achieved what most brands only dream of: it never truly lost a customer again. Because when you combine intelligence with empathy, automation with authenticity, and data with heart—you don't just build retention systems.

You build relationships that last forever.

Epilogue

The Future of Customer Retention

As we reach the end of this journey, it's important to pause and reflect on the transformative power of AI-driven customer retention. Throughout this book, you've learned the strategies, frameworks, and real-world stories that illustrate how predictive analytics, behavioral insights, and automated personalization can fundamentally change the way businesses connect with their customers. But beyond the tactics lies a bigger truth: customer retention is no longer optional—it's the defining factor of long-term success in the digital economy.

The businesses that thrive in the future will be the ones that understand people—not just as buyers, but as dynamic, evolving individuals with preferences, habits, and emotional responses. AI is not a replacement for human understanding; it is a magnifier. It gives you the ability to see patterns invisible to the human eye, anticipate needs before they arise, and deliver care consistently at scale. When applied thoughtfully, AI transforms customer retention from a reactive effort into a proactive, predictive, and personalized experience.

Looking ahead, the potential of AI in retention is limitless. Emerging technologies like natural language processing, advanced sentiment analysis, and real-time predictive modeling will continue to refine how businesses understand their customers. Future AI systems will not only predict churn or upsell opportunities—they will anticipate emotional states, identify engagement triggers, and create experiences that feel intuitive and human. The companies that adopt these tools early will not only retain customers—they will inspire loyalty, advocacy, and lifelong connections.

But technology alone is not enough. The stories in this book—from the coffee shops to online courses, from boutique brands to SaaS platforms—show that the human element is irreplaceable. Empathy, creativity, and authenticity must remain at the core of every AI-powered strategy. AI can automate processes, optimize timing, and personalize messaging, but it cannot create trust or foster genuine relationships on its own. The most successful businesses are those that use AI to amplify their humanity, not replace it.

It is also worth noting that retention is not a static achievement—it is a continuous journey. Every customer interaction, every message, every touchpoint is an opportunity to learn, adapt, and improve. By measuring the right metrics—churn probability, lifetime value, sentiment, and engagement—you can refine your strategies continuously. AI provides the tools to act faster, respond more intelligently, and optimize interactions at scale. The result is a living system that grows smarter over time, compounding the value of every customer relationship.

The principles you've learned here are applicable across industries, business sizes, and markets. Whether you run a small subscription business, an online education platform, or a global SaaS company, the AI retention framework scales. It allows you to deliver personalized experiences to thousands—or even millions—of customers without losing the sense of human connection. It turns data into insight, insight into action, and action into loyalty.

Finally, the ultimate takeaway from this book is simple: customer retention is the engine that powers sustainable growth. Acquisition alone will never build a resilient business. The future belongs to brands that combine intelligence, automation, and empathy to keep their customers not only engaged, but inspired. Every sale becomes the beginning of a relationship, every interaction an opportunity to strengthen trust, and every touchpoint a chance to deepen loyalty.

As you move forward, your challenge is to put these principles into practice. Build your AI retention systems thoughtfully. Monitor your metrics, anticipate your customers' needs, and continually refine your strategies. Most importantly, never lose sight of the human side of your business. When you do, you'll discover that retention is not merely about preventing loss—it's about creating experiences so meaningful, personalized, and consistent that customers choose to stay, advocate, and grow with you.

The future of business is not about the fastest growth or the largest ad spend. It is about the relationships you cultivate, the trust you build, and the experiences you deliver. AI is your tool, your guide, and your amplifier. Combined with care, strategy, and consistency, it transforms ordinary transactions into extraordinary, lifelong connections.

Welcome to the next era of customer retention—a world where your business anticipates, understands, and delights your customers at every stage. A world where relationships are engineered, nurtured, and multiplied. And most importantly, a world where your customers remain loyal not because they have to, but because they *want to*.

This is the power of AI-powered retention. This is the blueprint for sustainable, scalable, and human-centered growth. And now, it's your turn to implement it, adapt it, and watch your business evolve in ways you never thought possible.

The journey doesn't end here. It begins.

Printed by Libri Plureos GmbH in Hamburg, Germany